I'll Be Sober in the Morning

GREAT POLITICAL COMEBACKS, PUTDOWNS & RIPOSTES

EDITED BY
Chris Lamb

ILLUSTRATED BY
Steve Stegelin

FP
555-B Rutledge Avenue
Charleston, SC 29403
FRONTLINE PRESS LTD.

Illustrations by Steve Stegeglin

Layout and design by Fireball Media

Printed in the USA by United Graphics Incorporated of Mattoon, Illinois

Library of Congress Cataloge Number

2007927547

Christopher Jon Lamb, 1958 --

I'll be sober in the morning -- great political comebacks, putdowns and ripostes

ISBN 978-0-9723829-4-6

1. History. 2. Humor.

To Dan Quayle
for his many contributions to humor

PREFACE

John Wilkes, the eighteenth-century British political reformer, was engaged in an angry exchange with John Montagu, the Fourth Earl of Sandwich, who shouted, "Sir, I do not know whether you will die on the gallows or of the pox!" To which Wilkes responded, "That, sir, depends on whether I first embrace your Lordship's principles or your Lordship's mistresses."

There's no record of Montagu's response, or if he even had one. He probably put what was left of his manhood in a thimble and skulked away. To this day, no one has delivered a comeback so devastating and so spontaneous.

The ability to fire off a sharp riposte that leaves a rival red-faced and speechless can be a potent political weapon. In a war of words, however, not everyone is equal to John Wilkes, Winston Churchill, Abraham Lincoln, Benjamin Disraeli, or even Calvin Coolidge.

Churchill, who contributed the title and a number of the entries for this book, understood the secret behind the spontaneous putdown. "All the best off-the-cuff remarks," he said, "are prepared days beforehand."

To wit: In modern American politics, the best comeback belongs to the late Texas Senator Lloyd Bentsen, Michael Dukakis's running mate in the 1988 presidential election. Dukakis's opponent, the standing vice president George Herbert Walker Bush, had selected little-known Indiana Senator Dan Quayle as his running mate. The youthful Quayle tried to dismiss concerns about his inexperience by comparing himself to John F. Kennedy when JFK ran for president in 1960. Quayle's advisers cautioned him against bringing up the JFK comparison during his nationally televised debate with Bentsen.

Quayle ignored the advice, saying, "I have as much experience as Jack Kennedy did when he sought the presidency."

Bentsen was waiting: "Senator, I served with Jack Kennedy. I knew Jack Kennedy. Jack Kennedy was a friend of mine," Bentsen said calmly before landing the knockout punch. "Senator, you're no Jack Kennedy."

Bush and Quayle won the election. But Bentsen's putdown will forever be etched in American politics – and left Quayle forever tainted. After Quayle became vice president, a popular joke went: "The Secret Service has been ordered that if anything happens to President Bush, they are to immediately shoot Dan Quayle."

During the Cold War tensions of the late 1950s and early 1960s, Soviet Premier Nikita Khrushchev gained a reputation for pounding his shoe on the desk during United Nations debates – a traditional Russian custom of expressing displeasure with a speaker. When British Prime Minister Harold Macmillan addressed the U.N. General Assembly in 1960, he was aware Khrushchev would be present. At one point during Macmillan's speech, Khrushchev removed his shoe and started pounding. Unruffled, Macmillan turned to an interpreter and said, "Could I have that translated, please?"

Macmillan and Bentsen delivered their remarks before large television audiences, leaving no doubt what they had said. All politicians should be as considerate of those who edit books such as this.

It's possible, even probable, even likely, that some of the putdowns in this book were created after the fact, or perhaps created without fact. In my defense, I have taken the advice of many politicians: "Never let the facts get in the way of a good story."

When Jimmy Walker was mayor of New York, a political opponent trapped him in a lie. Asked by a reporter for a response, Walker just smiled and said, "Another good story ruined by an eyewitness."

Stories that were clearly apocryphal were not included in this book. For instance, New York Governor Thomas Dewey was the heavy favorite in the 1948 presidential election against Harry S. Truman. On Election Night, the story goes, Dewey asked his wife, "How will it feel to sleep with the president of the United States?" And she replied, "A high honor, and quite frankly, I'm looking forward to it." But Truman won the election and the next morning at breakfast, Mrs. Dewey said, "Tell me, Tom, am I going to Washington or is Harry coming here tonight?"

This book, is limited to political comebacks, putdowns, and ripostes. Therefore, any quip included here must be a response to something said or done.

This isn't a book of anecdotes, which are stories politicians often tell on the campaign trial to project the image of a favorite uncle while deflecting more serious issues. Unlike anecdotes, putdowns come from the dark side of the brain and are used as weapons. During one exchange between political rivals Nancy Astor and Winston Churchill, Ms. Astor snapped: "Winston, if you were my husband, I'd put poison in your coffee."

Churchill replied: "If you were my wife, Nancy, I'd drink it."

— Chris Lamb

In the fifth century BC, Alcibiades
debated his uncle, the Greek orator Pericles.
"When I was your age, Alcibiades,
I talked just the way you are now talking," Pericles said.
"If only I had known you, Pericles," his nephew said,
"when you were at your best."

A friend once said to Cato the Elder,
"It's a scandal that no statue has been erected to you
in Rome. I am going to form a committee
to see that this is done."
"No," Cato said, "I would rather have people ask,
'Why isn't there a statue to Cato?' than
'Why is there one?'"

The Roman statesman Metellus Nepos,
whose mother had a reputation for promiscuity,
once teased Cicero on the famous orator's low birth.
"Who, after all, was your father?"
Metellus Nepos asked Cicero.
"It would be much harder for me
to tell who yours was," Cicero replied.

King Henry VIII requested that Sir Thomas More carry a strongly worded note to King Francis I of France. More protested: “Your majesty, you know his temper. Why, he might even have me beheaded.”

“Never fear,” the monarch assured him. “If he does, I will have the head of every Frenchman in London.”

“This is most kind of your majesty,” More replied. “But I don’t think any of their heads will fit my shoulders.”

After the death of England's Protestant King Charles II in 1665, his Roman Catholic brother James II assumed the throne. Charles's illegitimate son, James Scott, the Duke of Monmouth, led an unsuccessful rebellion. The rebels were brought before Chief Justice George Jeffreys, known as "Hanging Judge Jeffreys." During one of the trials the notorious judge stuck his cane in the chest of one rebel, snarling, "There is a rogue at the end of my cane!" The defendant sneered, "At which end, my Lord?"

Eighteenth-century British playwright Richard Brinsley
Sheridan served for a number of years in the
House of Commons. A Liberal, Sheridan was a
frequent critic of the conservative Tories.
Strolling through Piccadilly Square,
Sheridan was approached by two English lords.
Each took a position beside him.
As the three continued walking, one of the lords said,
"I say, Sherry, we were just discussing whether
you were a rogue or a fool."
Sheridan answered,
"Why, I do believe I am between both."

A lady had hoped Richard Brinsley Sheridan would go for a walk with her. The feeling was not mutual and Sheridan tried to use the weather as an excuse. She observed that the weather had cleared sufficiently for them to take a stroll.

"It may have cleared up enough for one," Sheridan said, "but not enough for two."

When a clergyman asked British Prime Minister
George Canning how he enjoyed his sermon,
Canning replied, "You were brief."
"Yes," said the clergyman,
"you know I try to avoid being tedious."
"But," Canning replied, "you were tedious."

When Founding Father John Adams was informed he had become America's first vice president, he responded: "My country has, in its wisdom, contrived for me the most insignificant office that ever the invention of man contrived or his imagination conceived."

Friends told former President John Quincy Adams, then approaching eighty, that a young congressman was ridiculing him on account of his age.
"Tell that young man," the venerable politician responded, "that an ass is older at thirty than a man is at eighty."

When John Randolph of Virginia was delivering a speech on the floor of the House of Representatives, he was repeatedly interrupted by Philomen Beecher of Ohio, who would jump to his feet and call for "previous question, Mr. Speaker," a parliamentary maneuver to cut off debate on the pending question. After ignoring Beecher's first few interruptions, Randolph had finally had enough. "Mr. Speaker," he said, "in the Netherlands, a man of small capacity, with bits of wood and leather, will, in a few moments, construct a toy that, with the pressure of the finger and thumb, will cry, 'Cuckoo, Cuckoo.' With less ingenuity, and with inferior materials, the people of Ohio have made a toy that will, without much pressure, cry, 'Previous question, Mr. Speaker!'"

It was well known in the early 1800s that John Randolph was sexually impotent. Yet, few dared use that against him. Once, however, in the heat of a congressional debate, a rival made jest of Randolph's impotence.

A furious Randolph replied, "Sir, you pride yourself on an ability in which any barbarian is your equal and any jackass immeasurably your superior."

In the early years of Washington, D.C., the city was made up of wooden houses and muddy streets. Bitter rivals Congressman John Randolph of Virginia and Congressman Henry Clay of Kentucky met on a narrow plank. One would have to step into the mud. Randolph stood his ground and challenged Clay: "I will not give way for a scoundrel," he said. Clay bowed, smiled, and stepped off the board. "I will," he said.

While delivering a dull and lengthy address in Congress, General Alexander Smyth turned to Henry Clay and remarked: "You, sir, speak for the present generation, but I speak for posterity."
Clay responded: "Yes, and you seem resolved to speak until the arrival of your audience."

A woman reacted with disappointment that
Henry Clay had not remembered her name.
"No," Clay replied, "for when we last met long ago
I was sure your beauty and accomplishments
would very soon compel you to change it."

Henry Clay was sitting outside a Washington hotel with Massachusetts Senator Daniel Webster, when a man walked by with a pack of mules.

"Clay, there goes a number of your Kentucky constituents," Webster said.

"Yes," Clay replied, "they must be on their way to Massachusetts to teach school."

Daniel Webster, when offered the
vice presidency in 1828, indignantly replied,
"I do not propose to be buried until I am dead."

Soon after John Tyler succeeded William Henry Harrison as president, he sent his son Robert to order a special train. The railroad superintendent told the younger Tyler that he didn't run special trains for presidents.

"What!" Tyler exclaimed. "Didn't you furnish a special train for the funeral of General Harrison?"

"Yes," the superintendent said. "And if you will bring your father here in that shape, you shall have the best train on the road."

Before Alexander Hamilton Stephens became
vice president of the Confederacy, he was elected
from Georgia to the House of Representatives.
When fellow Whig Benjamin Hill accused him
of being a Judas to his party
by supporting slavery, Stephens repeatedly
challenged him to a duel. Hill repeatedly declined.
On one occasion, Stephens charged that Hill was
"not only an impudent braggart
but a despicable poltroon besides."
Hill still refused, saying, "I have a soul
to save and a family to support and you have neither."

In the course of a House debate, Representative
A.H. Stephens said, “My opponent is not fit to carry swill.”
Other congressmen cried out, “Order, order!”
and Stephens was told to apologize.
“Mr. Speaker, I do apologize,” Stephens said.
“The congressman is absolutely fit
for the duty to which I referred.”

When A. H. Stephens was in the Senate,
an angry opponent shouted at the diminutive Georgian,
"You little know-nothing, I could swallow you whole
and never know I had eaten anything."
Stephens fired back, "And if you did that, you would have
more brains in your belly than you have in your head."

As a young lawyer, Abraham Lincoln once had to plead two cases in the same day before the same judge. Both involved the same principle of law, but in one Lincoln appeared for the defendant; in the other, he appeared for the plaintiff.
In the morning he made an eloquent plea and won his case. In the afternoon Lincoln took the opposite side but argued it with the same earnestness.
The amused judge asked Lincoln what had made him change his argument.
"Your honor," Lincoln said, "I may have been wrong this morning, but I'm right this afternoon."

In 1846, Abraham Lincoln ran for Congress
against evangelist Peter Cartwright, who tried to turn
one of their debates into a revival,
addressing the crowd and saying,
"All who desire to give their hearts to God
and go to heaven, stand."
Many stood.
"All who do not wish to go to hell, stand,"
Cartwright continued.
And everybody but Lincoln stood.
"I observe that everybody but Mr. Lincoln indicated
he did not want to go to hell," Cartwright said.
"May I inquire of you, Mr. Lincoln, where are you going?"
Still seated, Lincoln said, "I am going to Congress."

An Abraham Lincoln speech was interrupted
by a heckler who yelled, "Do I have to pay a dollar
to see one of the ugliest men in the country?"
Lincoln answered, "I'm afraid so, sir,
that you were charged
a dollar for that privilege – but I have it for nothing."

During one of the Lincoln-Douglas debates, Senator Stephen Douglas called Abraham Lincoln "two-faced." Whereupon Lincoln replied, "I leave it to my audience. If I had another face, do you think I would wear this one?"

President Abraham Lincoln was constantly frustrated
by the indecisiveness of his top general,
George McClellan. Once, when Lincoln
visited McClellan's headquarters with an aide,
the general was nowhere to be found.
Lincoln heard hammering in the woods nearby.
He found some soldiers building something,
and he asked what it was.
"It's a new privy for the general," one of the soldiers said.
"Is it a one-holer or a two-holer?" Lincoln asked.
"A one-holer, sir," the soldier answered.
Once out of earshot of the soldiers, the president
told his aide, "Thank God it's a one-holer,
for if it were a two-holer, before McClellan could make up
his mind which to use, he would beshit himself."

During another of the Lincoln-Douglas debates, Stephen Douglas told their conservative audience that he had once seen Lincoln selling whiskey. When it was his turn to speak, Lincoln did not dispute the charge. He agreed that he had once worked as a bartender. "I was on one side of the bar serving drinks," he said, "and Douglas was on the other side, drinking them."

After Union General Joseph Hooker succeeded George McClellan, he sent President Abraham Lincoln a telegram informing him, "headquarters in the saddle." "The trouble with Hooker," Lincoln said, "is that he's got his headquarters where his hindquarters ought to be."

During the Civil War a friend tried to console
President Abraham Lincoln, saying,
"I hope that the Lord is on your side."
Lincoln replied that this was not his hope.
"My wish," he said, "is that I am on the Lord's side."

Pennsylvania Congressman Thaddeus Stevens
was reported to have said that Lincoln's
Secretary of War, Simon Cameron,
"would steal anything but a red-hot stove."
Cameron protested to Lincoln, who suggested to Stevens
that he might care to say he had been misquoted.
Stevens agreed and announced he had indeed been
misquoted. What he really said was that Cameron
"would steal anything, including a red-hot stove."

President Abraham Lincoln once had an adjutant general who repeatedly explained that he was late to meetings because his watch ran slow.

"Well," Lincoln said, "you must get a new watch or I must get a new adjutant general."

When one of President Abraham Lincoln's advisers
recommended a particular man for a post
in the cabinet, Lincoln shook his head.
Asked why, Lincoln said, "I don't like the man's face."
"But," the adviser protested, "the poor man
isn't responsible for his face."
Lincoln raised a finger and said,
"Every man over forty is responsible for his face."

A foreign diplomat walked into Abraham Lincoln's office
while the president was polishing his shoes.
"Mr. President!" the startled diplomat said with disdain,
"you black your own boots?"
"Yes," Lincoln said. "Whose boots do you black?"

A temperance committee visited
President Lincoln in late 1863 and asked him
to fire his top general, Ulysses S. Grant.
"For what reason?" Lincoln asked.
"Why?" the group's spokesman said.
"He drinks too much whiskey."
Lincoln paused, then said, "Well, I wish one of you would
tell me what kind of whiskey Grant drinks. I would like
to send a barrel of it to every one of my generals."

Former Secretary of State William Seward
and New York political boss Thurlow Weed
were riding up Broadway one day and passed the
bronze statue of Abraham Lincoln in Union Square.
Seward, who had lost the Republican nomination to
Lincoln in 1860, told Weed, "If you had stayed loyal to me,
I would have a bronze statue there instead of Lincoln."
Unapologetic, Weed responded, "Seward, is it not better
to be alive with me than dead in bronze?"

Brooklyn preacher Henry Ward Beecher
was an outspoken abolitionist. During the Civil War,
Beecher campaigned in support of the Union cause,
at one point visiting England
in his crusade against slavery.
While speaking in Manchester, he encountered
a hostile crowd of Southern sympathizers.
"Why didn't you whip the Confederates in sixty days,"
one heckler yelled, "as you said you would?"
Beecher, who knew the Revolutionary War was still
a sensitive topic for many in England, responded,
"Because we had Americans
to fight this time, not Englishmen."

When General Ulysses S. Grant expressed his contempt
for a certain officer, another general protested
that the man in question had been through ten campaigns.
"So has that mule, yonder," Grant snapped,
"but he's still a jackass."

In 1875, President Ulysses S. Grant officially opened the new State Department building, which was hideous in its architecture. A guide, who proudly gave Grant a tour, said, "One thing more, Mr. President. The building is fireproof."

"What a pity," Grant replied.

Shortly after the end of the Civil War, John Allen was running for Congress for the first time in Mississippi. The former army private found himself facing a former major, a couple of former colonels, and two or three former generals. Each of his opponents pulled rank on Allen, reminding their audience of their contributions to the South's losing effort. When it was Allen's turn, he said: "Now the officers are boasting of their accomplishments and making their appeal to you veterans. I simply ask that all of you who were generals vote for the generals; all of you who were colonels, vote for colonels; all of you who were majors vote for the major; but all of you ditch-digging enlisted men, you vote for Private John Allen." He was overwhelmingly elected and was thereafter known as "Private John Allen."

Congressman John Allen once was pleading his case before hostile voters. Someone in the audience threw a large rock at Allen, which passed over his head because he had stooped at that instant.

"You see," Allen told supporters who tended to him, "if I had been an upright politician, I would have been killed."

In the course of a conversation, a congressman
told newspaper editor Horace Greeley
that he was a self-made man.
“That, sir,” Greeley replied,
“relieves the Almighty of a great responsibility.”

Benjamin Disraeli, a Tory, and William Gladstone,
a Liberal, were intense rivals who each served as
prime minister of Great Britain.
During a debate in Parliament, Disraeli used the word
"calamity" but quickly substituted it with "misfortune."
Asked if there was really a difference between the two,
Disraeli said yes and he would explain by example.
"If my honorable friend Gladstone were accidentally
to fall into the Thames River, it would be a misfortune,"
Disraeli said, "but if anyone were to pull him out,
that would be a calamity."

Observing that Benjamin Disraeli had the reputation
for being able to make a joke about any subject,
William Gladstone asked if that were indeed true.
Disraeli said it was entirely possible.
"Then I challenge you," Gladstone said.
"Make a joke about Queen Victoria."
"Sir," Disraeli replied, "her majesty is not a subject."

A newly elected member of parliament went to
Benjamin Disraeli for advice.
"For the first six months," Disraeli told him, "you should
listen and not become involved in debate."
"But my colleagues will wonder
why I do not speak," the new MP protested.
"Better they should wonder why you do not,"
Disraeli said, "than why you do."

When a British voter insulted Benjamin Disraeli by telling him his wife had picked him out of the gutter, Disraeli answered, "My good fellow, if you were in the gutter no one would pick you out."

During one of his speeches, Benjamin Disraeli
was interrupted by a heckler who yelled,
"Speak quick! Speak quick!"
Disraeli responded: "It is very easy for you to
speak quickly; you only utter stupid monosyllables,
but when I speak I must measure my words. I have to
open your great thick head. What I say is to enlighten you.
If I bawled like you, you would leave this place
as great a fool as you entered it."

During another speech, a heckler interrupted
Benjamin Disraeli by yelling, "Speak up! I can't hear you."
Disraeli answered, "Truth travels slowly,
but it will reach you in time."

A colleague complained to Benjamin Disraeli
that his attacks on John Bright, a Liberal member
of the House of Commons, were too harsh.
"After all," he said, "John Bright is a self-made man."
Disraeli replied, "I know he is and he adores his maker."

Suffragist Julia Ward Howe tried to enlist
Massachusetts Senator Charles Sumner
in the case of a person who needed help.
"Julia, I've become so busy I can no longer
concern myself with individuals," Sumner said.
Howe replied, "Even God hasn't reached that stage yet."

After President James Garfield was wounded
by an assassin's bullet, he lay on his death bed for weeks,
restricted to a diet of oatmeal and lime water.
When Garfield was told that the great
Indian Sitting Bull was starving himself in captivity,
Garfield snapped, "Let him starve."
A moment went by, and the president added,
"Better yet, send him my oatmeal."

U.S. Supreme Court Chief Justice Melville W. Fuller was presiding at a church conference when an audience member rose and began a tirade against universities and education, saying that he gave thanks to God that he had never been corrupted by any contact with a college.

"Do I understand the speaker thanks God for his ignorance?" Fuller interrupted.

"Well, yes, if you want to put it that way," the man answered.

"Then," Fuller replied, "you have a great deal to be thankful for."

When a congressman quoted Henry Clay, saying,
"I would rather be right than president," Speaker of the House Thomas Brackett Reed replied,
"He need not to worry. He will never be either."

When asked if the Republicans would nominate him for president, Thomas Brackett Reed said, "They could look much farther and do much worse. And I think they will."

When the Reverend Edward Everett Hale
was chaplain of the U.S. Senate, he was asked
if he prayed for the Senators.
"No," he said. "I look at the Senators
and pray for the country."

An angry senator once directed his fury
at fellow Senator George Vest of Missouri,
denouncing him viciously on the Senate floor.
When the attack ended, Vest rose slowly and said,
"After listening to the remarks of my learned colleague,
I feel somewhat like the little corporal in the Philistine
army, who, after Samson had passed through,
picked himself off the ground and,
holding his battered head, cried out, 'Now I know
what it feels like to be smitten by the jawbone of an ass.'"

When influential New York politician Roscoe Conkling was asked why he refused to campaign for the corrupt James G. Blaine, the Republican presidential candidate in 1884, he responded, "I don't engage in criminal practice."

During the 1900 presidential campaign between Democrat William Jennings Bryan and Republican William McKinley, a Democratic speaker announced confidently that Mrs. Bryan would be sleeping in the White House after Inauguration Day. The Bryan supporter was interrupted by a Republican, who yelled, “If she is, she’ll be sleeping with McKinley.”

When Martin Dies Sr. of Texas was considering
a run for Congress, he sought the advice
of a former Texas governor.
The old politician told Dies to tell voters that he
supported more subsidies for farmers, larger pensions for
veterans, and increased assistance for the poor, but that he
would also be frugal with taxpayers' money.
"But, governor," Dies protested, "if I advocate
all of those spending measures and at the same time
call for curbs in spending, don't you think the people
will think me inconsistent?"
The governor answered: "Martin, the people
don't think, and if they ever started,
they wouldn't elect you to Congress anyway."

Virginia Senator Claude Swanson delivered a speech that exceeded its allotted time. As Swanson was leaving the hall an elderly woman shook his hand. Swanson responded by asking how she liked the speech. "I liked it fine," she said, "but it seems to me you missed several excellent opportunities." "Several excellent opportunities for what?" asked Swanson. "To quit," the woman said.

Learned Hand, the distinguished New York
appellate judge, argued a point of law with his friend
Justice Oliver Wendell Holmes.
"But," Judge Hand said,
"we're talking about a court of justice."
"No," Holmes said, "it's only a court of law."

In 1904, Republican presidential candidate
Theodore Roosevelt was addressing a rally when he was
interrupted by a drunk who yelled, "I am a Democrat!"
When Roosevelt asked why, the man replied,
"Because my grandfather was a Democrat
and my father was a Democrat."
TR patiently nodded and said to the man,
"Let me ask you, sir. If your grandfather had been
a jackass and your father had been a jackass,
what would you be?"
"A Republican!" the drunk shot back.

While a friend was visiting President Theodore Roosevelt
in the White House, TR's young daughter Alice
kept pestering them.
"Mr. President," the friend complained,
"isn't there anything you can do to control Alice?"
Roosevelt replied, "I can do one of two things.
I can be president of the United States
or I can control Alice. I cannot possibly do both."

In 1910, President William Howard Taft asked
former President Theodore Roosevelt to represent
America at the funeral of King Edward VII of England.
While in London, Roosevelt ran into
German Kaiser Wilhelm II. The Kaiser invited
Roosevelt to call on him the next day, adding,
"Be there at two o'clock sharp,
for I can only give you forty-five minutes."
Unwilling to be patronized, the former president replied:
"I will be there at two o'clock sharp,
but unfortunately I have just twenty minutes to give you."

New York Senator Chauncey Depew looked at
President William Howard Taft's girth and asked what Taft
and his wife intended to call the child when it was born.
"If it's a girl, I shall name it for my wife.
If it's a boy I will call him Junior," Taft said.
"But if it is, as I suspect, just gas,
I will call it Chauncey Depew."

At dinner one night, Chauncey Depew joined a small group of friends who were in the midst of a spirited discussion.

"Oh, Mr. Depew! You're just in time to settle an argument," one of the ladies in the group said. "What is the most beautiful thing in the world?"

"A beautiful woman," Depew responded.

"I contend," the woman scoffed, "that sleep is the most beautiful."

"Well," Depew answered, "next to a beautiful woman, sleep is."

Opera singer Mary Gordon
had a figure to match her magnificent voice.
Upon seeing her in a gown with a pronounced
décolletage, a smitten Chauncey Depew
asked her what kept her dress up.
“Two things,” she replied,
“your age and my discretion.”

Chauncey Depew once introduced diplomat
Joseph Choate at an after-dinner speech by saying that
if you opened Choate's mouth and dropped in a dinner,
a speech would come up.
Choate then came to the microphone and said,
"Mr. Depew says that if you open my mouth
and drop in a dinner, up will come a speech.
But I warn you that if you open your mouths and drop in
one of Mr. Depew's speeches, up will come your dinners."

When longtime Boston Mayor James M. Curley
was speaking during one of his many political campaigns,
a heckler shouted,
"I wouldn't vote for you if you were St. Peter."
Curley shot back, "If I were St. Peter,
you wouldn't be in my precinct."

Champ Clark of Kentucky was
Speaker of the House of Representatives when an
Indiana congressman named Johnson interrupted
the speech of an Ohio congressman, calling him a jackass.
Clark ruled the expression to be in violation
of parliamentary procedure and Johnson apologized.
"I withdraw the unfortunate word, Mr. Speaker,
but I insist the gentleman from Ohio is out of order."
"How am I out of order?" the Ohioan asked.
"Probably a veterinarian could tell you,"
the Indiana congressman answered.

British Prime Minister David Lloyd George
increased the size of the British army and ordered an
increase in the production of weapons.
Lloyd George's critics created a committee to
investigate the accusations of overspending.
When the committee issued its highly critical report,
one of Lloyd George's ministers observed,
"I suppose, sir, that means the end of your program."
"No," Lloyd George snapped,
"it means the end of the committee."

Upon being introduced to the Welsh-born
David Lloyd George, an obnoxious Londoner
loudly remarked so that he could be heard by others,
"I had expected to find Mr. Lloyd George
a big man in every sense, but you see for yourself
he is quite small in stature."
"In North Wales we measure a man
from his chin up," Lloyd George replied.
"You evidently measure from his chin down."

In the early days of World War I,
Kaiser Wilhelm II of Germany was talking
to the head of the Swiss army.
"You have an army of only 500,000 men.
What would you do if attacked by an army
of one million men?" the Kaiser snidely asked.
"Each one of our soldiers," the Swiss officer answered,
"would simply have to shoot twice."

At the beginning of World War I, Kaiser Wilhelm II asked Belgium King Albert I for permission to march his army through Belgium on its way to attack France. "I rule a nation," Albert snapped, "not a road."

When Woodrow Wilson was governor of New Jersey,
he was informed that one of the state's U.S. senators
had died and it would be Wilson's responsibility
to appoint a replacement.
Shortly thereafter, a state politician called
Wilson and said, "Mr. Governor,
I'd like to take the senator's place."
"It's okay with me," Wilson replied,
"if it's okay with the undertaker."

President Woodrow Wilson became an invalid
after his stroke in 1919. Republican legislators,
including Senator Albert B. Fall, suspected that
Wilson's wife, Edith, was running the country.
Fall and a delegation of his colleagues showed up
unannounced at the White House one afternoon.
However, they found Wilson in bed but hardly enfeebled.
An unnerved Fall told Wilson,
"Mr. President, I am praying for you."
Wilson responded, "Which way, Senator?"

At the Versailles Peace Conference in 1919,
French statesman Georges Clemenceau held out for the harshest terms against Germany. Someone pointed out that historians would be arguing for generations over who was responsible for starting the Great War.
"Yes," Clemenceau said, "but one thing is certain:
They will not say that Belgium invaded Germany."

At a conference of the League of Nations
after World War I, Ignacy Paderewski of Poland
and French Prime Minister Georges Clemenceau
met for the first time.
“You are the great pianist?” Clemenceau asked.
Paderewski bowed.
Clemenceau continued, “And now you are
the premier of Poland?”
Again Paderewski bowed.
“My, my,” said Clemenceau, with a sigh.
“What a comedown.”

As a young man, French statesman
Georges Clemenceau fought a number of duels.
On one occasion he traveled with his second
to a Paris railway station and bought a one-way ticket.
"A one-way ticket?" his companion said. "Pessimistic?"
"Not at all," Clemenceau said. "I always use my opponent's
return ticket for the trip back."

Lady Margot Asquith, the wife of
British Prime Minister Herbert Asquith,
was introduced to Jean Harlow, the American actress.
Harlow kept mispronouncing Lady Asquith's first name as
MAR-gut, as if it rhymed with "harlot."
"My dear," Lady Asquith explained,
"the 't' is silent, as in Harlow."

In 1921, Agnes Macphail became the first woman
elected to the Canadian House of Commons.
Not all of her colleagues welcomed her.
One of her male colleagues once pointedly asked her,
"Don't you wish you were a man?"
"No," Macphail replied. "Don't you?"

During a meeting with President Warren Harding, whose administration was tainted with scandal, comic Will Rogers said, “I would like to tell you all the latest jokes, Mr. President.”

“You don’t have to,” Harding answered. “I appointed them all to office.”

When Calvin Coolidge was president
of the Massachusetts Senate, two senators
got into a bitter exchange in which one
told the other to go to hell.
The recipient of the remark demanded that
Coolidge come to his defense.
"I've looked up the law, Senator," Coolidge told him,
"and you don't have to go."

When Calvin Coolidge was vice president,
his successor as governor of Massachusetts,
Channing Cox, paid him a visit.
Cox asked how Coolidge had been able
to see so many visitors when he was governor,
yet always left the office by 5 p.m.,
while Cox found he often stayed in his office as late as 9.
"Why the difference?" Cox asked.
Coolidge replied, "You talk."

Aviator Charles Lindbergh tried to urge President Calvin Coolidge to fly in an airplane. "Mr. President, it's the safest mode of passenger transportation. In 200,000 passenger miles, only one casualty," Lindbergh said. Coolidge replied, "That's very little comfort for the casualty."

One evening a nervous soprano struggled hopelessly before President Calvin Coolidge at a White House recital. “What do you think of the singer’s execution?” one of the guests asked Coolidge. “I’m all for it,” the chief executive replied.

Senator George H. Moses stormed into the
White House during the Coolidge Administration
to complain that a man under consideration
for a senatorial nomination was "an SOB."
"That could be," Coolidge conceded,
"but there are a lot of those in the country, and I think
they are entitled to representation in the Senate."

Senator Jim Watson of Indiana bluntly gave his constituents his opinion on an issue. He then added, "Now you have the facts, and you know exactly where I stand on the issues. You can vote for me, or you can go to hell." When Calvin Coolidge heard this, he remarked, "He gave them a difficult alternative."

After a conference with a foreign ambassador, reporters asked President Calvin Coolidge if he had anything to say. "No," Coolidge said. "And I have nothing to say about anything else either."
As the reporters were leaving, Coolidge called out, "And don't quote me."

Soon after Calvin Coolidge became vice president, he received a dinner invitation. Coolidge's secretary checked the Social Registry but couldn't find the name of the host.

"No conclusion can be drawn from that," Coolidge said. "I've only been in it myself for a half hour."

Sitting next to President Calvin Coolidge at a White House dinner, a woman opened a conversation with the man known as Silent Cal. "Mr. President, I've made a bet that I can make you say at least three words. What do you have to say?"

"You lose," Coolidge said.

When someone teased Calvin Coolidge for his habitual silence, he replied, “Well, I found out early in life that you never have to explain something you haven’t said.”

Calvin Coolidge arrived home from church
when his wife, who had been too ill to attend,
inquired about the subject of the minister's sermon.
"Sin," Coolidge said.
"And what did he say about it?"
Mrs. Coolidge inquired.
"He was against it."

President Calvin Coolidge was annoyed
by fellow Republican Senator William Borah of Idaho,
who often criticized the administration.
One day while horseback riding, an aide pointed to
another rider and asked, "Isn't that Senator Borah?"
"Can't be," Coolidge said. "The rider and the horse
are going in the same direction."

After Calvin Coolidge announced he would not run for a second term, reporters pressed him for more details. “Exactly why don’t you want to be president again, Mr. Coolidge?” one reporter asked. “Because there’s no chance for advancement,” Coolidge said.

Calvin Coolidge's successor, Herbert Hoover,
was president when the Great Depression seized America.
Just before the 1932 election, actor Otis Skinner
told Coolidge, "I wish it were you that
we were going to vote for in November.
It would be the end of our horrible depression."
"And it would be the beginning of mine,"
Coolidge replied.

When Jimmy Walker was mayor of New York, a political opponent trapped him in a lie. The reporters asked Walker what he had to say. With nowhere to hide, Walker smiled and said, "Another good story ruined by an eyewitness."

While attending a University of Illinois homecoming football game, writer Ring Lardner jumped out of his seat when the school's military honor guard fired a salute as Governor Len Small entered his box.

"What the hell was that about?" Lardner asked.

"For the governor," someone told him.

"Good heavens!" cried Lardner. "They missed him."

Between World War I and World War II,
Mohandas Gandhi led his campaign of civil disobedience
to win India's independence from the British Empire.
In 1931, Gandhi traveled to London to meet with British
authorities. He was constantly swarmed by reporters and
photographers and peppered with questions.
One day a reporter shouted, "What do you think
of Western civilization?"
"I think it would be a good idea," Gandhi replied.

When Huey Long was governor of Louisiana,
he kidded Texas Governor James "Pa" Ferguson,
"If there had been a back door at the Alamo,
there wouldn't have been a Texas."
"But there was a back door," Ferguson replied,
"and that's why there's a Louisiana."

A political opponent charged New York Governor Al Smith with telling lies about him. "You ought to be glad," Smith replied. "If I told the truth about you, they'd run you out of town."

Governor Al Smith once implored a taxi driver
to hurry to a radio station for a broadcast.
The driver, not recognizing his passenger,
begged to be excused, saying he was anxious to get home
in time to hear the governor's address over the radio.
Smith offered the cabbie
a handsome tip and urged him to drive.
"Hop in mister," the driver said, reaching for the money.
"To hell with the governor."

Al Smith was delivering a campaign speech
when someone in the audience yelled,
"Tell us all you know, Al. It won't take long!"
To which Smith replied, "Better yet, I'll tell them all
we both know, and it won't take any longer."

As a rookie reporter for the New York World,
Heywood Broun went to interview
Utah Senator Reed Smoot.
"I have nothing to say," Smoot told Broun.
"I know," replied Broun.
"Now let's get down to the interview."

Heywood Broun and another newspaperman
were listening to a politician give a speech that
was full of distortions and outright lies.
"He's murdering the truth,"
the newspaperman told Broun.
"Don't worry," Broun said.
"He'll never get close enough to do it any harm."

After another big year, New York Yankees slugger Babe Ruth went to team owner Jacob Ruppert and demanded a raise to $80,000 for the next season. The shocked owner tried to reason with him, pointing out that $80,000 was more than President Herbert Hoover made.

"Yes," Ruth said, "but I had a much better year than he did."

Writer Dorothy Parker and
U.S. Representative Claire Booth Luce
bumped into each other entering a restaurant.
"Age before beauty," Luce sniffed, stepping aside.
"And pearls before swine,"
answered Parker as she walked past.

Early in his career, Winston Churchill
left the Conservative Party to join the Liberals and grew a moustache, hoping to look older and more distinguished.

One day, a female constituent ran into Churchill on a London street and disdainfully remarked, "Mr. Churchill, I approve of neither your politics nor your moustache."

"Don't worry, Madam," Churchill replied, "you are unlikely to come in contact with either."

Winston Churchill had been drinking heavily
at a party when he bumped into Bessie Braddock,
a Socialist member of Parliament.
"Mr. Churchill, you are drunk," Braddock said harshly.
Churchill paused and said, "And Bessie, you are ugly.
You are very ugly. I'll be sober in the morning."

American-born Lady Nancy Astor was the first woman
to take a seat in the British House of Commons,
where she was the object of great antagonism from many
members, including Winston Churchill.
Churchill told Astor he found her intrusion
into the all-male society as embarrassing
as if she had burst into the bathroom.
"Winston," she said, "you are not handsome enough
to have worries of that kind."

In the House of Commons, Lady Astor
was in debate on agriculture when Winston Churchill
interrupted to question her knowledge of farming.
"I'll make a bet she doesn't even know how many
toes a pig has," Churchill said.
Lady Astor replied, "Why don't you take off
your little shoesies and we'll count them together?"

During an exchange in Parliament, Lady Nancy Astor told Winston Churchill, "Winston, if you were my husband, I would put poison in your coffee."
"If you were my wife, Nancy,"
Churchill replied, "I would drink it."

Worried about Winston Churchill's eccentric behavior,
one Parliament member confided to Lady Astor,
"We just don't know what to make of him."
"How about a nice rug?" she suggested.

Playwright George Bernard Shaw invited
Winston Churchill to the premiere of a new play,
enclosing two tickets:
"One for yourself and one for a friend – if you have one."
Churchill wrote back, saying he couldn't make it, but
maybe he could have tickets for the
second night – "if there is one."

While listening to a member of the opposition party in the House of Commons, Winston Churchill began shaking his head, eventually receiving more attention than the speaker.

Realizing he was being upstaged, the speaker turned to Churchill and snapped, "I wish to remind the right honorable friend that I am only expressing my own opinion."

Impishly Churchill replied, "And I wish to remind the speaker that I am only shaking my own head."

Winston Churchill was approached by an admirer
who said, “Doesn’t it thrill you, Mr. Churchill,
to know that every time you make a speech the
hall is packed to overflowing?”
“It is quite flattering,” Churchill admitted.
“But whenever I feel this way I remember
that if instead of making a political speech,
I was being hanged, the crowd would be twice as big.”

When Winston Churchill showed a friend
a group of paintings he had recently completed,
the friend asked him why he painted only landscapes
and never portraits.
Churchill replied, “Because a tree doesn’t
complain that I haven’t done it justice.”

The conservative Winston Churchill was often at odds with Clement Attlee, leader of the Labor Party, which advocated a greater role for the government in economic policy. Churchill once entered a men's room to find Attlee standing at the urinal. Churchill took a position at the other end of the trough. "Feeling standoffish today, are we, Winston?" Attlee asked. "That's right," Churchill responded. "Every time you see something big, you want to nationalize it."

FOR A
GOOD TIME,
CALL BESSIE
BRADDOCK

A speaker was well along in his boring address
on the floor of the House of Commons
when he observed Winston Churchill napping.
"Must you fall asleep while I'm speaking?"
the speaker demanded.
"No," said Churchill, eyes remaining shut.
"It's purely voluntary."

When someone said to Winston Churchill that
Clement Attlee, then the prime minister,
was a modest man, Churchill agreed, adding,
“But then he does have a lot to be modest about.”

Clement Attlee had supported Winston Churchill
during World War II but often disagreed with Churchill
and his imperiousness during cabinet meetings.
During one meeting, Attlee attempted to
raise a matter for discussion.
Churchill dismissed him by saying that
the topic had been discussed in a previous meeting.
Attlee, impatient with Churchill's long-winded lectures,
remarked, "A monologue is not a discussion."

When Winston Churchill delivered his famous Iron Curtain Address at Westminster College in Fulton, Missouri, in 1946, a ceremony was held to dedicate a bust of the wartime prime minister. After the ceremonies were over, a buxom woman approached Churchill and gushed, "Mr. Churchill, I traveled over a hundred miles this morning for the unveiling of your bust."

Churchill replied, "Madam, I assure you that I would gladly return the favor."

When staying at the White House as a guest
of President Franklin Roosevelt, Winston Churchill
was coming out of his bath when FDR
entered Churchill's room.
Startled upon seeing the naked Churchill, FDR reversed
his wheelchair, but he was stopped when Churchill said,
"The Prime Minister of Britain has nothing to hide
from the President of the United States."

At a White House luncheon in 1943, Winston Churchill was angrily confronted by Helen Reid, wife of the anti-British owner of the Chicago Tribune, who assailed the prime minister for British treatment of Indians during its colonization of the subcontinent. Churchill coolly responded: "Before we proceed further, let us get one thing clear. Are we talking about the brown Indians of India, who have multiplied under benevolent English rule? Or are we speaking of the red Indians in America who, I understand, are almost extinct."

While in America, Winston Churchill was invited to
a buffet luncheon where cold fried chicken was served.
Returning for a second helping, he asked politely,
"May I have some breast?"
Overhearing this, his hostess scolded him.
"Mr. Churchill, in this country we ask for white meat
or dark meat." Churchill apologized.
The following morning, Churchill sent the lady
a magnificent orchid with a note that read, "I would be
most obliged if you would pin this to your white meat."

On Winston Churchill's eightieth birthday,
a young man was sent to take his photograph.
The photographer, awestruck to be in the presence of Churchill, stammered, "Sir Winston, it is wonderful to take your photograph on your eightieth birthday and I do look forward to taking it again on your hundredth birthday."
Churchill replied, "Young man, you appear to me in good health and sound in wind and limb.
So I see no reason why you should not."

The rotund Queen Salote Tupou, of Tonga,
was present for the coronation of Queen Elizabeth II
in 1953. The ceremonies dragged on throughout the
morning and into the afternoon. When the portly
Queen Tupou passed by where Churchill was sitting,
she was followed by a small boy.
Churchill was nudged by a companion
who pointed to the boy and asked, "Who's that?"
"Her lunch," Churchill grumbled.

Well into his eighties, Winston Churchill
periodically attended the House of Commons.
As he was helped down the aisles by two aides,
one young MP said to another, “You know, I don’t think
he should come in anymore, he’s getting so dottery.”
The other then whispered: “Yes, and they say
he’s even getting a bit soft in the upper story.”
And then Churchill added, “And they also say
that he’s getting hard of hearing.”

One day when Winston Churchill was in his eighties,
it was tactfully pointed out to him that his fly was open.
The elder statesman snapped,
"Dead birds don't fall out of nests."

In the washroom of his London club,
newspaper publisher Lord Beaverbrook bumped into
Edward Heath, a young member of
Parliament and future prime minister, whom Beaverbrook
had insulted in an editorial a few days earlier.
Embarrassed by the encounter, Beaverbrook said,
"My dear chap, I've been thinking it over and I was wrong.
Here and now, I wish to apologize."
"Next time," Heath said, "I wish you'd insult me
in the washroom and apologize in your newspaper."

In 1934, President Franklin Delano Roosevelt
named financier Joseph P. Kennedy chairman
of the new Securities and Exchange Commission.
Democratic National Chairman Jim Farley protested the
appointment, telling FDR of the unscrupulous methods
Kennedy had used to build his fortune. FDR held firm,
telling Farley that he had good reason for putting
Kennedy in charge of Wall Street.
"You set a thief to catch a thief," FDR said.

One morning First Lady Eleanor Roosevelt
left the White House to visit a prison in Baltimore.
When her husband Franklin Roosevelt awoke later, he
asked Mrs. Roosevelt's secretary where his wife was.
"She's in prison," Mrs. Roosevelt's secretary said.
"I'm not surprised," FDR replied, "but what for?"

In 1935, a French diplomat suggested to Soviet leader Josef Stalin that he might warm frosty relations with the Vatican if he were to show more tolerance to Catholics. To this suggestion, Stalin replied, "How many divisions does the Pope command?"

When told of Stalin's answer, Pope Pius XI replied, "You may tell my son Josef he will meet my divisions in heaven."

Artist Pablo Picasso lived in Paris during the German occupation in World War II. Nazi authorities regarded Picasso as a Communist sympathizer and routinely harassed him.

During one investigation, a Nazi officer looked at a photograph of Picasso's anti-war painting, Guernica. The mural – over 25 feet in width – depicts the German destruction of the Basque town of Guernica in 1937.

Pointing at the photograph, the Nazi officer asked brusquely, "Did you do that?"

"No!" Picasso snapped. "You did."

When Frank Knox was Secretary of the Navy
during World War II, a friend asked him a casual question
about the movement of certain ships in Atlantic waters.
The question was thoughtless and Knox
leaned over and said, “Can you keep a secret?”
“Of course, I can,” the friend replied eagerly.
“Well,” said the secretary, “so can I.”

Dr. Robert Oppenheimer, who supervised the creation of the first atomic bomb, was asked by a congressional committee if there was any defense against the weapon. "Certainly," Oppenheimer replied. "The defense is peace."

Asked if he would appoint Labor Leader John L. Lewis ambassador to the United Nations, President Harry Truman said, “I wouldn’t appoint him dogcatcher.” When he heard that, Lewis said, “Of course he wouldn’t. Because if he did, he’d have more brains in the dog department than in the State Department.”

After being elected governor of California,
Earl Warren opened a speech by saying,
"I'm pleased to see such a dense crowd here tonight."
"Don't be too pleased, governor!" a voice shouted.
"We ain't too dense!"

Former Georgia Governor Herman Talmadge
was asked what would be the effect of all the people
moving from Georgia to Florida.
"I am sure it will enhance the level of intelligence
of both states," Talmadge said.

After Alban Barkley, vice president during
Harry S. Truman's administration, gave a speech,
he sat down next to a friend and said,
"What did you think of my speech?"
"Well," his friend answered, "I have only three criticisms.
First, you read it. Second, you read it poorly.
Third, it wasn't worth reading."

During the 1951 Australian elections,
Prime Minister Arthur Fadden appeared at a town hall.
His speech was interrupted by a member of the audience
who yelled, "Why don't you lazy politicians
who live off us do a fair day's work?"
Fadden, clearly irritated, replied, "Look, my friend,
I work while you're asleep."
"Of course you do," someone else in the audience fired
back. "We all know you're a burglar."

Someone asked Senator Margaret Chase Smith of Maine,
"What would you do if you woke up
and found yourself in the White House?"
"I would go to the President's wife," Mrs. Smith said,
"apologize and then leave at once."

At the end of a speech, New York Representative
Emanuel Celler was approached by a female admirer
who asked if she might have his notes as a souvenir.
The Congressman said that he had no notes.
She said she would be satisfied with
a transcript of the address.
But no transcript had been made, Celler explained.
"Do you think there's any possibility of your speech
being published?" the woman persisted.
"Maybe posthumously," replied Celler jokingly.
"Well," she said, "let's hope it's soon."

When future congressman Robert T. Stafford
was serving Vermont as attorney general in the 1950s,
he argued a case before the state Supreme Court.
In the course of his argument, Stafford could not
persuade the chief justice to his point of view.
Finally, he said, "Mr. Chief Justice, I shan't pursue
this line of argument any further, as obviously there is
no use in banging my head into a stone wall."
The chief justice replied, "No, Mr. Attorney General.
There isn't, but I know of no one who could do so
with less fear of personal injury than you."

During an interview, a reporter asked
British Prime Minister Harold Macmillan,
"Sir, what do you think is the real meaning of life?"
"Good god!" Macmillam replied. "If you want to know
the meaning of life, see your archbishop.
Don't ask a politician."

During tensions between the Soviet Union and the West
in 1960, Soviet Premier Nikita Khrushchev had
the reputation for pounding his shoe on the table
in the U.N. General Assembly – a traditional
Russian custom of expressing displeasure with a speaker.
When British Prime Minister Harold Macmillan stood
to address the General Assembly, he was ready
as Khrushchev's obnoxious pounding began.
Turning to an interpreter, he said,
"Could I have that translated, please?"

British Labor Leader Aneurin "Nye" Bevan once asked Harold Wilson, his successor as prime minister, "Were you really born in Yorkshire?"

"Not just born, Nye," Wilson said proudly. "Forged."

Bevan responded, "I always thought there was something counterfeit about you."

French President Charles de Gaulle emerged unharmed after 110 bullets were fired at his car in an assassination attempt. "Those people really aim very badly," de Gaulle said.

A French citizen approached President Charles de Gaulle and said, “My friends are not content with your policies.” “Well,” de Gaulle answered, “change your friends.”

American statesman and two-time presidential candidate Adlai Stevenson was approached by an enthusiastic woman supporter during one of his losing campaigns against Dwight Eisenhower.

"Governor," she said, "every thinking person will be voting for you."

"Madam, that is not enough," Stevenson replied. "I need a majority."

While Adlai Stevenson was campaigning in California,
a woman asked him where he had gotten his deep tan.
"Have you been playing golf?" she asked sternly.
"No," Stevenson said. "I got this tan
making outdoor speeches in Florida."
"Well," the woman told him, "if you got that brown,
you talked too long."

In Dallas in 1963 for a United Nations Day speech, U.N. Ambassador Adlai Stevenson was interrupted repeatedly by a heckler who challenged the ambassador to state his beliefs.

Stevenson ignored the first few interruptions, then looked toward the heckler and said, "I believe in the forgiveness of sin and the redemption of ignorance."

During a speech at the United Nations,
U.S. Ambassador Henry Cabot Lodge found himself
constantly interrupted by the Soviet ambassador.
Lodge finally turned to the Russian and inquired why
"the gentleman" kept demanding the floor.
"I am not a gentleman. I am the representative of the
Soviet Union," the ambassador answered sharply.
"The two are not mutually exclusive," Lodge replied.

Vice President Richard Nixon faced
Senator John F. Kennedy during the
1960 presidential election. Nixon was completing
two terms as Dwight Eisenhower's vice president,
yet Eisenhower said little to endorse Nixon.
A reporter asked Eisenhower to provide an example
of how Nixon had contributed to the administration
during his eight years in office.
Ike paused for a long moment, then said,
"If you give me a week, I might think of one."

After hearing John F. Kennedy's inaugural address in 1961, Richard Nixon, who had narrowly lost to Kennedy, bumped into Ted Sorenson, one of JFK's speechwriters, and said, "I wish I had said some of those things."
"What part?" Sorenson asked. "The part about, 'Ask not what your country can do for you ...'?"
"No," Nixon said. "The part that starts, 'I do solemnly swear...'"

Early in his term, John F. Kennedy was asked by a reporter, “If you had to do it over again, would you run for the presidency and would you recommend the job to others?” “Well,” replied JFK, “the answer to the first is yes, and the answer to the second is no. I don’t recommend it to others, at least not for a while.”

Flying in Air Force One, President John F. Kennedy
was asked by a reporter what would happen
if the airplane crashed.
"I'm sure of one thing," Kennedy said. "Your name would
be in the paper the next day, but in very small print."

In the 1950s, U.S. senators began installing phones
in their cars as a symbol of status.
When Republican Minority Leader Everett M. Dirksen
got his phone, he immediately called
Majority Leader Lyndon Johnson.
"Lyndon," he said smugly, "I just got a car phone.
I thought I'd make my first call to you."
"Just a minute, Ev," Johnson replied,
"while I answer my other phone."

During the Democratic primaries of 1960, Senator Lyndon Johnson and his family believed that LBJ would ultimately be the party's nominee for president. But at the convention in Los Angeles, the nomination went to John F. Kennedy. Johnson would, instead, be JFK's running mate. Johnson's mood darkened when one of his daughters was late returning from Disneyland. As the Johnsons hurried for the convention, LBJ groused, "We didn't come out here to see Disneyland." "I know," his daughter answered dejectedly. "But we didn't come out here to see you run for vice president either."

Joseph Kennedy, the father of John F. Kennedy,
once remarked to JFK of his granddaughter Caroline,
"Caroline's very bright, smarter than you were,
Jack, at that age."
"Yes, she is," JFK agreed.
"But look who she has for a father."

President John F. Kennedy
was speaking with a conservative industrialist.
"You know," JFK said, "if I weren't President,
I'd be buying stocks now."
"Yes," said the businessman. "And if you weren't President,
I'd be buying stocks now, too."

President Lyndon Johnson had a reputation
for verbally abusing his staff. On at least one occasion
Press Secretary Bill Moyers got the last word.
After Moyers delivered grace over dinner,
LBJ complained to Moyers that he couldn't hear him.
"Mr. President," replied Moyers,
"I wasn't speaking to you."

There were rumors that President Lyndon Johnson
would select as his running mate Robert Kennedy,
the brother of the man whose assassination
had made LBJ president.
A reporter asked Robert Kennedy,
"How do you feel about a Johnson-Kennedy ticket?"
RFK answered, "I'd be willing, but I'm not sure
Mr. Johnson would accept the vice presidency."

Australian Prime Minister William McMahon's balding pate, quivering voice and mild demeanor made him vulnerable to criticism. McMahon once complained to Liberal Parliament Member James Killen,

"I'm my own worst enemy."

Killen replied, "Not as long as I'm alive."

In 1978, mild-mannered Tory minister Sir Geoffrey Howe attacked the budget proposals of Labor Leader Denis Healey on the floor of the House of Commons. Healey responded, “That part of the speech was rather like being savaged by a dead sheep.”

In 1981, as President Ronald Reagan was recuperating in his hospital bed after the assassination attempt on his life, an aide tried to reassure Reagan that the government was functioning normally. Reagan, who had been in good spirits, immediately became agitated and snapped: "What makes you think I'd be happy about that?"

When Ronald Reagan ran for a second term in 1984, he was in his 70s and critics questioned his vitality for the office. During a television debate between Reagan and his Democratic Party challenger Walter Mondale, a reporter raised the issue of age to Reagan.

"I want you to know that I will not make age an issue of this campaign," Reagan replied. "I am not going to exploit for political purposes my opponent's youth and inexperience."

Walter Mondale lost to Ronald Reagan
in a landslide in 1984. Several years later,
Mondale was asked how long it took to recover.
"I'll let you know when the grieving ends," Mondale said.

During a television debate against incumbent
South Carolina Senator Fritz Hollings in 1986,
Republican candidate Henry McMaster
challenged his opponent to take a drug test.
"I'll take a drug test," Hollings said,
"if you'll take an IQ test."

The three living former presidents Jimmy Carter, Gerald Ford, and Richard Nixon stood side by side at a White House reception during the Reagan Administration. Observing the three standing together, Senator Bob Dole said, "There they are. See no evil, hear no evil, and . . . Evil."

In 1984, Democratic presidential candidates
met in a forum to present their qualifications.
Ohio Senator John Glenn talked at length about
his historic orbit around the earth as an astronaut in 1962.
When it was his turn to respond, Senator Fritz Hollings
turned to Glenn and said:
"But what have you done in this world?"

The so-called "Koreagate Scandal" of the late 1970s
involved the South Korean government's alleged bribery
of dozens of senators and congressmen.
On a segment of ABC's This Week, television journalist
Sam Donaldson, who wore an artless hairpiece,
tried to unnerve Senator Fritz Hollings
by asking him where he got the
Korean suit he was wearing.
"Sam, if you want to personalize it,"
Hollings snapped, "I got it right down the street
from where you got that wig."

Senator Fritz Hollings found himself
in an elevator with the diminutive Senator John Tower,
of Texas, who puffed out his chest to show Hollings
the expensive suit he had just purchased.
"What do you think?" Tower gushed.
"Does it come in men's sizes?" Hollings quipped.

During a 1988 debate among Democratic presidential candidates, Missouri Representative Richard Gephardt was rambling at length with an anecdote from his childhood. At one point Gephardt mentioned that his mother used to give him castor oil every morning.

Two of the other candidates, Senator Al Gore and Jesse Jackson, were sitting next to each other when Gore whispered to Jackson, "Jesse, when you were a boy, did your mother give you castor oil?"

"No," Jackson replied, "but I wasn't full of shit."

When television reporter Andrew Kirtzman
was interviewing New York Mayor Ed Koch,
he pressed the mayor on an issue.
Koch, clearly frustrated, leaned closer to the reporter
and said, "I can explain this to you;
I can't comprehend it for you."

When reporters asked President
George Herbert Walker Bush to display the middle finger
from which he was about to have a cyst removed,
Bush replied, “Don’t tempt me.”

In 1988, George Herbert Walker Bush selected little-known Senator Dan Quayle as his running mate. The youthful-looking Quayle tried to deflect concerns about his age and inexperience by comparing himself to John F. Kennedy. Quayle's handlers told him not to bring up the comparison during his debate with the Democratic vice presidential candidate Lloyd Bentsen. But Quayle ignored the advice. "I have as much experience," Quayle said at one point, "as Jack Kennedy did when he sought the presidency." Bentsen turned to Quayle and said, "Senator, I served with Jack Kennedy. I knew Jack Kennedy. Jack Kennedy was a friend of mine. Senator, you're no Jack Kennedy."

Vice presidential candidate Lloyd Bentsen
was asked why he and his running mate Michael Dukakis
did not carry Bentsen's home state of Texas
during the 1988 presidential election.
"I just wasn't able to convince voters that
'Dukakis' was Greek for 'Bubba,' " Bentsen said.

In 1981, before Dan Quayle served as Vice President, he joined a group of congressmen for a weekend golf outing. The group was accompanied by a well-endowed female lobbyist looking to trade sex for votes. The scandal threatened Quayle's political ambitions until his wife, Marilyn, said that she knew her husband had done nothing inappropriate on the trip. "Anyone who knows Dan," she said, "knows that he would rather play golf than have sex any day."

After the 1992 Republican
National Convention, Vice President Dan Quayle declared
that he planned to be “a pit bull”
in the upcoming campaign
against the Democratic presidential candidate
Bill Clinton and his running mate Al Gore.
When Clinton heard the news, he said,
“That’s got every fire hydrant in America worried.”

Vice President Dan Quayle complained publicly
after satirist Garry Trudeau poked fun of him
in the comic strip Doonesbury.
"It's well known that Garry Trudeau
has a personal vendetta against me," Quayle said.
In response, the late-night talk-show host
Johnny Carson said, "Vice President Quayle is mad at
Garry Trudeau for satirizing Quayle in his comic strip.
That's the way to get through to Quayle – make fun of him
on the comic page; he's bound to see it."

When Democratic Governor Robert Casey
of Pennsylvania was running for re-election in 1990,
he made a campaign stop in a small town
in the state's largely Republican northwest corner.
"Hi, I'm running for governor," Casey told the
gas station attendant who was filling his car's gas tank,
"and I'd like to have your vote."
There was an awkward pause. Finally, the attendant
looked up and said, "Yes, I'll vote for you."
Relieved, Casey asked why.
"Because," the attendant said, "anybody would be better
than the guy they have in there now."

In July 2000, presidential candidate George W. Bush
told reporters on board his campaign plane,
"I don't read half of what you write."
"We don't listen to half of what you say,"
one of the reporters responded.
Bush replied, "That's apparent in the half of what I read."

Speaking to the media after a meeting with
Russian President Vladimir Putin, President
George W. Bush said that he had told Putin
he wanted to see a more democratic Russia.
"I talked about my desire to promote institutional change
in parts of the world, like Iraq where there's a free press
and free religion," Bush told reporters. "I told him
that a lot of people in our country would hope
that Russia would do the same."
When Putin spoke, he reminded everyone of the chaos
and violence that had resulted in the U.S attempt to instill
a democracy in Iraq. "We certainly would not have
the same kind of democracy as Iraq," Putin said.

Chris Lamb is a professor of Communication at the College of Charleston in Charleston, S.C., where he teaches journalism. His writing has appeared in *The New York Times, Los Angeles Times, Philadelphia Inquirer, Christian Science Monitor, Newsweek* and *Sports Illustrated.*

This is his fourth book. His other books include *Blackout: The Untold Story of Jackie Robinson's First Spring Training*; *Drawn to Extremes: The Use and Abuse of Editorial Cartoons*; and *Wry Harvest: An Anthology of Midwest Humor*. He lives in Charleston, S.C., with his wife Lesly and son David.

I hope you have enjoyed reading my book, *I'll Be Sober in the Morning*, as much as I enjoyed researching and compiling it. If you did, please tell your friends about it.

Do you have a comment or criticism? Share it with me and other readers at http://SoberInTheMorning.blogspot.com

And if you have heard a good comeback, putdown or riposte lately, I'd like to see that, too. Thanks.